TAE KWON DO

Paul Mason

SEA-TO-SEA

Mankato Collingwood London

This edition first published in 2011 by
Sea-to-Sea Publications
Distributed by Black Rabbit Books
P.O. Box 3263, Mankato, Minnesota 56002

Printed in China, Dongguan

Library of Congress Cataloging-in-Publication Data

Mason, Paul, 1967-
  Tae kwon do / Paul Mason.
     p. cm. -- (Combat sports)
  Includes index.
  ISBN 978-1-59771-277-4 (library binding)
  1. Tae kwon do--Juvenile literature. I. Title.
  GV1114.9.M37 2011
  796.815'3--dc22

                          2009051539

9 8 7 6 5 4 3 2

Published by arrangement with the Watts Publishing Group Ltd, London.

Series editor: Adrian Cole
Art director: Jonathan Hair
Design: Big Blu
Cover design: Peter Scoulding
Picture research: Luped Picture Research

Acknowledgments:
20th Century Fox / The Kobal Collection / Richard Cartwright: 4; Colombia / The Kobal Collection: 7; Desmond Boylan /
Reuters / Corbis: 29; Embassy / The Kobal Collection: 19; Guang Niu / Reuters / Corbis: 25; ImageState / Alamy: 13;
Joe Patronite / Getty Images: 29; Lee Jae-Won / Reuters / Corbis: 12; Lifestyle Photography: 10, 11, 15, 16, 17, 26, 27;
Matt Towler: 20; PA Photos / AP Photo / Al Behrman: 24; PA Photos / AP Photo / Edgard Garrido: 22, 23; PA Photos /
AP Photo / Julie Jacobson 14; Photo12.com / Collection Cinema: 6; Reuters / Action Images: 28; Reuters / Enrique
Marcarian: 1, 5, 11; Reuters / Lee Jae Won: 9; Reuters / Stringer: 18; Rogue Pictures / The Kobal Collection: 8; Zhang
liwen / Imaginechina: 21

Every attempt has been made to clear copyright. Should there be any inadvertent omission please apply to the
publisher for rectification.

Please note: The Publishers strongly recommend seeking professional advice and training before taking part in
contact sports. The Publishers regret that they can accept no liability for any loss or injury sustained.

March 2010
RD/6000006414/002

CONTENTS

WHAT IS TAE KWON DO?

What do *Buffy the Vampire Slayer* and a South Korean general have in common? The answer is the combat sport tae kwon do!

To Sunnydale, from Korea

The high kicks and punches Buffy used to fight Sunnydale's vampires come from tae kwon do. Tae kwon do is a Korean fighting style, founded in 1955 by General Choi Hong Hi.

One of the reasons Sarah Michelle Gellar got the part of Buffy the Vampire Slayer was that she was already a brown belt in tae kwon do.

"Destructo girl. That's me."
Sarah Michelle Gellar in Buffy the Vampire Slayer.

Competition Tae kwon do

Tae kwon do is a competitive sport. It features in the Olympics, and tae kwon do World Championships are held regularly. Most towns and cities have tae kwon do clubs.

Kicks are one of the main moves in tae kwon do. They allow attacks to be made from farther away than punches, and are more powerful.

Self Defense

Competitive sportspeople are not the only ones who learn tae kwon do. Others learn it as a way of defending themselves if attacked. A well-placed kick to the head scares off all but the most determined bully or mugger!

FOOT, FIST, DISCIPLINE

What does the word "tae kwon do" mean? In Korean:

* *tae* = foot
* *kwon* = fist
* *do* = discipline.

So, tae kwon do is the discipline of foot and fist.

ANCIENT MARTIAL ARTS

Ancient tomb paintings of warriors show that martial arts have been used in Korea for centuries. Tae kwon do is the descendant of these martial arts.

Japan Invades

In 1910, Korea was invaded by Japan. The Japanese banned Korean martial arts and anyone caught using them was punished. Some people continued to practice in secret.

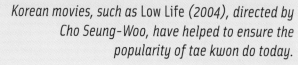
Korean movies, such as Low Life (2004), directed by Cho Seung-Woo, have helped to ensure the popularity of tae kwon do today.

Tae kwon do is Born

Japanese forces left Korea in 1945. Traditional Korean martial arts could be used in the open once more. In the 1950s, General Choi Hong Hi of the South Korean army joined the different martial arts forms together and called them tae kwon do.

THE WRECKING CREW

The 1970s action movie star Chuck Norris is a tae kwon do black belt. He first appeared in the 1969 Dean Martin movie *The Wrecking Crew* (right). His kicks and punches added spice to the spoof spy movie.

Ideals of Tae kwon do

Tae kwon do was founded with three key ideals
   * that a strong body and mind make it possible to stand up for justice
   * that the friendship that comes from taking part in tae kwon do is open to everyone
   * that all tae kwon do students should work toward a peaceful and fair world.

SPREADING AROUND THE WORLD

Tae kwon do soon began to spread around the world. One of the things that made the sport increasingly popular was its use in movies.

Tae kwon do and the Movies

Tae kwon do's spectacular kicks, spins, and punches were used by movie stars. They made the stars look tough—even if most of them weren't actually tae kwon do experts!

This chop kick is from the movie *Fearless*, which starred Jet Li.

Increasing Popularity

Inspired by the spectacular action they saw at the movies, people around the world began taking tae kwon do lessons. In 1973, the first-ever World Championships were held. Then, at the 2000 Olympics, tae kwon do became a full Olympic sport for the first time.

The South Korean Special Weapons and Tactics (SWAT) team performs a tae kwon do demonstration. Events like this help promote tae kwon do.

JOSEPH HAYES

Joseph Hayes was captain of the U.S. team at the first tae kwon do World Championships in 1973. He was also friends with action movie stars such as Bruce Lee. Hayes helped tae kwon do to spread in the United States and around the world.

"Joe Hayes shook the world!"
Grandmaster Henry Cho, Tae kwon do Hall of Fame.

TOP 10 TAE KWON DO MOVES 1—4

Kicks are the most powerful moves in tae kwon do. They allow fighters to attack from a distance, and with greater force than a punch.

1 The Turning Kick

The turning or "roundhouse" kick is a powerful kick that is often used in movies because it is so spectacular.

1. Here, the student is going to kick with his right foot. He starts with his right foot back and his right leg more bent than his left.

3. As his body turns away and back, his right foot comes around from the side, accelerating as his leg straightens.

2. Now he pushes his right hip forward and puts all his weight on his left leg. His right knee comes up and slightly inward, leading the right foot.

2 Front Kick

The front kick is often taught in self-defense classes. It is a fast kick, and can be used to kick an attacker anywhere, from the shin to the head.

3 Side Kick

One of the most versatile kicks in tae kwon do, the side kick can be used for attacks and to block an opponent's attack. The side kick can be used going forward, skipping to the side, or jumping up. From any of these positions, it is extremely powerful.

4 Chop (Axe) Kick

The chop kick is one of the most powerful and dangerous kicks in tae kwon do. It requires great speed and flexibility. The foot comes up quickly and then down in a "chop" action.

THE DISCIPLINE OF TAE KWON DO

Tae kwon do is a tough sport. Students are expected to be mentally and physically hard, and to dedicate themselves to their studies.

Breaking

One of the ways advanced fighters show their toughness is through "breaking"—spectacularly smashing up thick pieces of wood, concrete, brick, and other hard things.

"Breaking" is a popular spectator event. It requires great skill and speed.

"Notice that the stiffest tree is most easily cracked, while the bamboo or willow survives by bending with the wind."
Bruce Lee, martial-arts legend.

Sparring

Sparring is the kind of practice that is closest to a real fight. Two students practice techniques together. Sparring can sometimes be completely "free," with none of the practice moves planned.

Here tae kwon do students are practicing poomsae. They hope their movements will become automatic reactions.

Poomsae

In *poomsae*, tae kwon do students repeat the same moves over and over again. Their bodies eventually learn to do the movements automatically, without thought. This is very useful in a competition or for self-defense.

TAE KWON DO WORDS

These Korean words are often heard in the practice studio:

* *Cha-ryot* = attention
* *Gyong-rye* = bow
* *Jun-bi* = ready
* *Shi-jak* = begin
* *Hae-san* = dismiss
* *Ki-hap* = yell (usually at the end of an attack. The "h" is nearly silent, so it sounds like: "Ki-up.")
* *Gal-ryeo* = break
* *Gyae-sok* = continue
* *Swi-eo* = at ease
* *Geu-man* = finish

FIT MIND, FIT BODY

Physical skills are only part of tae kwon do. Students are also expected to think in a positive way, and to reflect credit on their sport.

Tae kwon do Character

Tae kwon do students are expected to develop modesty, politeness, loyalty, humility, respect for other people, and trust in others. They are taught to bring this character to every aspect of their lives—not only to the practice studio.

A tae kwon do student practices in a shady corner of Central Park in New York. For many people, tae kwon do is a way of life.

"Try not... DO, or DO NOT. There is no 'try'."
Yoda, in Star Wars: The Empire Strikes Back, *trying to explain a very tae kwon do-like attitude to Luke Skywalker.*

THE BOW

Tae kwon do fighters do not watch each other as they bow. To do so would be to show a lack of trust in their opponent's honesty.

It is important for students to learn respect from an early age.

Benefits of Tae kwon do

One of the biggest benefits of learning to do tae kwon do is you are able to defend yourself if attacked. But there are other benefits as well:

* increased physical fitness
* more self-confidence
* better self-control
* increased determination
* better concentration.

Many tae kwon do students even find that their marks at school improve as they practice harder.

TOP 10 TAE KWON DO MOVES 5–7

Tae kwon do punches can be very powerful if done well. They rely on an opposite action from the nonpunching hand, which is drawn back as the punch goes forward.

5 Forward Punch

The forward punch and the reverse punch are two basic punches in tae kwon do. They both use a similar technique, but in the reverse punch, the opposite foot goes forward. The reverse punch is the more powerful of the two.

1. A forward punch with the right hand starts with the right foot back and the right fist on the hip. The left arm is up in front of the body.

2. The student steps well forward on to his right foot, whipping the left arm back as the right arm punches forward. His body twists forward, adding power to the punch.

6 Backfist Side Strike

This strike is used at close range for striking to the side. It is a useful move for people to learn for self-defense. The strike starts with the arms across the body, which is good for protection. Then the strike whips forward as the other arm is quickly drawn back.

7 Backfist Front Strike

This is a version of the side strike, but the attack goes forward and down, instead of coming in from the side.

MODERN TAE KWON DO

Many people who have tae kwon do lessons have been inspired by the high-kicking action from the Olympics. To reach Olympic standard takes great skill and years of determination.

Tae kwon do Training

Students of tae kwon do are separated into different ability groups, so that no one is overpowered and hurt during sparring. Fighters are also separated by weight, for the same reason.

These tae kwon do students in China are preparing for a grading exam. They train hard every day—even at school.

"I have no idea what my body feels like when it's not bruised, sore, or stiff."
Sarah Michelle Gellar, Buffy actress.

BELT COLORS

White is the belt worn by beginners, black by the experts. The belt colors are sometimes given meanings:

* White—the purity of a new student
* Yellow—the earth from which a plant sprouts and takes root
* Green—the plant's growth
* Blue—the skies toward which the plant grows
* Red—something that is dangerous
* Black—the opposite of a beginner's white.

"Whatever luck I had, I made. I was never a natural athlete, but I paid my dues in sweat and concentration and took the time necessary to… become world champion." *Chuck Norris, martial-arts star and 8th-dan tae kwon do black belt (after black belt grades go up in "dans").*

Chuck Norris (right) kicks his way out of trouble in An Eye For An Eye. He has starred in many martial-arts movies.

Grades and Promotion

Students are promoted to a higher grade after passing a grading exam. To pass, they have to demonstrate new techniques well. Getting promoted can be a lengthy process—there are set time limits before you can move onto the next level.

CLUBS AND DOJANG

The only way to learn how to do tae kwon do is to join a club with a qualified instructor. This will ensure you learn the techniques safely and well.

Dojang

The places where tae kwon do is practiced are called *dojang*. Some *dojang* are permanent, housed in a special space. Many other *dojang* are temporary, set up for classes in badminton or basketball courts.

It is important for students to have a good practice partner. Students gain more by training hard with maximum effort.

"If training is hard, winning will be easy, but if training is easy, winning will be hard."
Norman Harris, martial-arts expert.

A Typical Lesson

A typical tae kwon do lesson goes something like this:

* warmup, which can include tough physical exercise such as pushups;
* practicing basic moves, perhaps as *poomsae*;
* working with a partner to improve basic technique;
* practicing advanced techniques;
* warming down (stretching).

The International Taekwon-do Federation is one of many tae kwon do organizations that oversee clubs.

RULES OF THE DOJANG

* Bow when entering and leaving.
* Be polite.
* Keep your *dobok* (training uniform) clean.

* Always arrive on time.
* Never interrupt a teacher.
* Do not brag or boast.

TAE KWON DO COMPETITION

Tae kwon do competitions take place at every level, from club contests to the Olympics, World Championships, and Asian Games.

Parts of a Competition

In most tae kwon do competitions, there are contests for sparring, breaking, and *poomsae*. In sparring, fighters wear head and body protectors. The body protector is called a *hogu*. In breaking and *poomsae*, there is no need to wear protection.

Fighters do not have to wear body protection during poomsae competitions.

Rounds

Sparring competitions last three rounds. Colored belts fight 1-minute rounds with a 30-second rest between. Black belts fight 2-minute rounds with a 1-minute rest.

Scoring

The winner is the fighter with the most points:

✳ one point for an attack on the body protector;

✳ two points for an attack on the head;

✳ one point if a punch is thrown and stops the opponent in their tracks;

✳ one additional point if the opponent is knocked down and the referee counts;

✳ knockouts win the fight if the referee finishes a count of ten.

A WHACK ON THE HEAD

Different organizations have different rules about blows to the head:

✳ in the Olympics and World Taekwondo Federation fights, kicks to the head are allowed, but not punches;

✳ the International Tae kwon do Federation allows kicks and punches to the head (and a *hogu* is not worn).

TAE KWON DO AT THE OLYMPICS

In 1988, the Olympics were held in Seoul, the capital city of South Korea. Tae kwon do was part of the Games for the first time, as a demonstration sport.

Full Olympic Sport

Tae kwon do became a full Olympic sport for the first time in Sydney 2000. South Korea hoped to win all of the eight gold medals, but the very first gold was won by an Australian, Lauren Burns! Even so, South Korea went on to win three of the eight golds.

Knockout Blows

The bouts at the Olympics are thrilling. Many competitors aim to score a knockout by hitting their opponents with powerful kicks to the head. Even though the fighters wear head protectors, knockouts are still common.

Pascal Gentil of France (red) leaps before kicking Ibrahim Kamal of Jordan. Gentil won the Olympic bronze medal at Athens 2004.

SUDDEN DEATH AT THE OLYMPICS

If a fight at the Olympics is drawn, an extra "sudden-death" round of up to two minutes takes place. The first fighter to score wins.

"I feel such a great honor to receive the first Olympic medal for our country."
Tran Hieu Ngan, winner of Vietnam's first-ever Olympic medal, in any sport, when she won a tae kwon do silver in 2000.

Quoc Huan Nguyen of Vietnam (red) kicks Russia's Seyfula Magomedov. Nguyen won the match.

TOP TEN TAE KWON DO MOVES 8—10

Without defensive moves, or "blocks," tae kwon do contests would soon be over. Blocks allow fighters to stop an attack, and can provide opportunities for defenders to launch attacks of their own.

8 Cross-Hand Block

The cross-hand block is one of tae kwon do's most powerful defenses against kicks. The aim of the block is to stop the attack dead, not to deflect it. Because the arms are crossed, the rear arm can support the front arm in absorbing the force of the attack.

9 Low Block

The low block is a good defense against someone trying to kick to the groin. The block starts in a sideways stance, with the wrists crossed in front of the neck. As the kick comes in, the rear arm snaps back and the front arm snaps forward, toward the knee. This should force the kick harmlessly away.

10 Inward Block

The inward block defends against attacks to the chest and stomach. The defender twists her whole body around, using her forearm to deflect the attack.

FAMOUS FIGHTERS

There have been many great tae kwon do champions.
These are just a few of the most famous.

1 Kim Kyong-Hun

✳ One of the most successful modern tae kwon do fighters, Kim Kyong-Hun was captain of the South Korean team at the 2000 Sydney Olympics.

✳ His Olympic record included gold at the 1992 Barcelona Olympics, which made him the first-ever heavyweight champion in tae kwon do's Olympic history. (Tae kwon do was still a demonstration sport in 1992.)

✳ Kim also won gold medals at tae kwon do World Championships in 1993, 1995, and 1997, and won gold at the 2002 Asian Games.

Kim Kyong-Hun of South Korea kicks out during the final of the thirteenth Asian Games. Kim went on to win the match.

2 Arlene Limas

* Arlene Limas of the United States was the first woman to win an Olympic gold for tae kwon do, when it was a demonstration sport in 1988.
* Limas was also selected as one of the top fighters of the twentieth century by *Tae Kwon Do Times* magazine.

Arlene Limas wins gold at the 1988 Olympic Games in Seoul, South Korea.

3 Chen Zhong

* China's Chen Zhong was the first woman ever to win tae kwon do gold medals at two Olympic Games, in 2000 and 2004.
* Both victories were convincing: in 2000, she won 8–3, and in 2004, 12–5.

Chen Zhong holds up her gold medal after winning the over 148 pound (67 kg) category.

GLOSSARY

banned
Made illegal or not allowed officially.

bouts
Combat sports contests between two fighters.

capital city
A city where the government of a country or region is based.

deflect
Push aside. Most blocking techniques in tae kwon do aim to deflect attacks.

demonstration sport
A sport at the Olympics that is not yet an official part of the Games, but is being given a trial run before possible inclusion in the future.

discipline
Self-control and dedication.

flexibility
Ability to bend your body, arms, and legs easily in all possible directions. Someone who can bend over and touch their toes without bending their knees is often said to be flexible.

founded
Begun or started.

groin
The area from the tops of your legs to the bottom of your stomach.

humility
The quality of being modest (not boastful) and respectful toward others.

ideals
Important principles about how to behave and treat other people.

invaded
Taken over by the armies of another country or area.

justice
Fairness.

knockout
A punch or kick that makes it impossible for a fighter to continue in the next ten seconds.

loyalty
Continuing to support someone through good or bad times.

martial arts
Different fighting sports.

modesty
Not showing off or boasting about your achievements, but instead keeping them quiet.

South Korea
A country in Asia, founded in 1948. Its neighbor is North Korea: until 1948 the two countries were one.

spoof
Pretend or not serious.

FURTHER INFORMATION

BOOKS

There are many instructional books about tae kwon do, where you can learn more about some of the techniques described in this book. The only way to really learn, though, is to join a tae kwon do club.

Taekwondo: A Step-by-Step Guide To The Korean Art Of Self-Defense

Master Kevin Hornsey (Connections, 2002)
One of the best instructional books about tae kwon do, where you can learn more about the Top 10 techniques shown in this book, and lots more besides.

Taekwondo For Kids

Y.H. Park (Tuttle Publishing U.S., 2005)
Aimed specifically at children, this book uses cartoons to demonstrate techniques.

DVDs

Taekwondo 1–Basic Training

Does what you'd expect: shows basic tae kwon do techniques for young people new to the sport.

MOVIES

Some of these movies are not suitable for all ages:

Good Guys Wear Black (Ted Post, 1978)

Chuck Norris, star of this movie, continued in the entertainment industry with a series of movies showcasing his trademark side kick (*The Octagon*, 1980, *Lone Wolf McQuade*, 1983).

Hong Kil Dong (Kil In Kim, 1986)

This historical drama, based on Korea's version of Robin Hood, was made in North Korea. The opening fight scene with a team of Japanese ninja is fantastic. Perhaps surprisingly, it was one of the most popular movies ever in Bulgaria in the late 1980s.

Best of the Best (Robert Radler, 1989)

The fictional adventures of a U.S. team heading for the tae kwon do World Championships.

Taekwondo (Seung-Wook Moon, 1998)

The story of a Korean named Kim, who settles in Poland and runs a tae kwon do class there. The film is also known as *Ibangin*.

WEB SITES

http://usa-taekwondo.us/

The Team USA Olympic web site tae kwon do section has photos and videos with team news and a picture archive of past events and champions. A directory of coaches helps you find someone to train with, and you can find out which events are taking place worldwide.

www.wtf.org

The home page of the World Taekwondo Federation. Here you can find out more about big competitions and *poomsae*, plus there are links to tae kwon do associations in all parts of the world.

www.youtube.com/results?search_query= taekwondo+breaking&search=Search

Hours of footage of experts using various parts of their bodies to break tiles, bricks, and other hard objects.

INDEX